# The Black Woman's 7 Day Guide to Self-Love

## Learning to Love Yourself One Day at a Time

# by
# Abril Smith

for Abrea and Abrianna whom I love with all
my heart!

# *Acknowledgments*

As I take the time to sit and reflect; it was just six months ago that I released my first book, "#College Rule". Since then I have held numerous book signings and have been invited to many different events to promote my work. For all of those who thought of me in any way I am truly grateful. None of this would be possible without God on my side. All I have, to Him I owe. One of the main reasons this second book was so important to me was because I wanted to break the cycle of being a one hit wonder. So many great writers, with works far better than my own have been reduced to only putting out one book. There are so many stories in my head that I want to tell and I thank God that he has spared no good thing by giving me such ample opportunities.

To my gorgeous daughters, you two have made me who I am and I am forever grateful that God chose me to be a mother to you. The late nights, the tears, the blood and sweat are all for you. You two are my heart! Mom and Dad none of this would be possible without you. Thank you for your continued guidance and reassurance. I know the sky is the limit with you two by my side. Love is an understatement, I carry you two in my heart with me wherever I go. To my brothers, what more can I say; *y'all* are still ugly but I love you! Aunt Judy, you are more than an aunt, you are a second mother, my doctor, my boss because you have made sure I stayed on task at all times.  Thank you for the gentle pushes and nudges, I love you!

When I published "#College Rule" there were so many people who reached out to me with a plethora of kind words and encouragement.  I cannot name all of you but Kiara, Mrs. Cooper, and Mrs. Sonya just to name a few—your kind words really meant the world to me!

XOXO,
Abril

# Let Me Holla At You?

I set out on a journey to write this book after a

ten year period of verbal, mental and physical abuse

at the hands of people I thought had my best interests at heart. If you know me personally, you would know that one of the biggest flaws that I claim to possess is having a big heart. As a medical professional, I feel the need to explain that in the medical field this condition is very dangerous and life-threatening, however, the big heart that I am referring to is my ability to try to see the good in others despite any preconceived notions I may have or have heard. I was always one to give others the benefit of the doubt, conversing and befriending known liars and thieves, not wanting to believe the things others said about them until they lied on me or stole from me. If you lie down with dogs, you are bound to get fleas!

To some extent not much has changed. Even in my adulthood, I still allow others to show me their true colors rather than believing the hype. As a result I have had my feelings trampled upon like brush under the hooves of a heard of wild horses. My heart has been broken more than once and in many different places, I have been made a fool of and perhaps worst of all, I have been let down. While taking the time to examine myself, putting my big heart and foolish ways of thinking on trial the jury came back with a unanimous verdict: GUILTY ON ALL CHARGES!

I was guilty of not ensuring others treated me the way I deserved to be treated. I was guilty of putting my feelings on the back burner to ensure the needs of others had been met. I had busied myself building up everyone and everything around me while my happiness sat in ashes and my mental health laid in ruins. My inner most being was hollow and desolate, my self-confidence had fled, I was destitute of the happiness that I had gone out of my way to afford to others.

The things that will be shared in this book are life lessons from my perspective as well as some of my closest friends. These are all things that I wished others would have shared with me or told me, perhaps preventing some of the terrible experiences I have had over the years. No, this book is not designed to prevent trouble from knocking on your front door, but it is my sincere hope and prayer that when trouble rears its ugly head, the lessons taught in the pages to come will have taught you to stand up for yourself, to value your feelings and to not allow negativity to harden your heart.

If you, like me have been found guilty on all charges of not allowing your full light to truly shine. If you have been convicted of not putting your best foot forward for fear of leaving others behind. If you have settled for less than what you were promised or what you deserved. If you, like me have allowed people to pick and pull at you until there is barely anything left, then keep reading, this book is most definitely for you!

# The Tea

In this society of hyper sensitivity I feel it is necessary to make some things clear before we begin. I, in no way, shape or form identify as a FEMINIST nor do I support their agenda. Feminism is just another way to keep us divided and the already unleveled playing field as a race. From a distance, the first very thing that others will see is the color of your skin, as they grow closer only then can they make and determine your gender. I say that to say this: In the eyes of all; we are BLACK FIRST and people later. I cannot allow myself to adopt the wicked and perverse practices of feminism and attack my own men and other women, blaming them for all the things wrong in our society.

A statement of this magnitude is bound to raise some eyebrows and throw many into a tizzy fit. I may very well lose some readers for my thoughts but the truth shall set you free. A feminist's agenda is disturbing and deeply rooted in the agenda of white supremacy in an effort to keep black men out of the home. The government convinced the black woman that she did not need her husband in the home to help raise the children, so she fought with him and drove him away. In return they give her a place to stay, to keep her content and quiet in the slums of housing projects with low rent. Subsidies in the form of food stamps are issued, keeping her reliant and dependent on the government for food. When her sons and daughters get out of line the government prefers to chastise them, stripping away her parental rights, calling simple correction and discipline child abuse and neglect.

If my views on this topic label me as a "pick me" then so be it. It is a badge that I will wear proudly if need be. At the end of the day we are all one race. History shows that no matter good, bad, right or wrong the opposite race always sticks together. This does not happen in the black community and for obvious reasons. How can we ever expect to be on a level playing field, demanding justice as a race when we bicker and fight amongst ourselves? Our opponents are playing chess and we are in the corner shooting marbles, WAKE UP!

This book is aimed at uplifting and encouraging the **BLACK WOMAN**. I can imagine the look of confusion and shock on your faces so allow me to pose the question I am sure you are all dying to know. Why do **BLACK WOMEN** need encouraging or uplifting? Well, I am so glad you asked! You see the very essence of the **BLACK WOMAN** as we know her is on the verge of extinction. Sounds like a ghastly thing to say but it's the truth! We are the most targeted, endangered, hunted, belittled, discouraged, and preyed upon human beings this world has ever seen. Crimes against us have gone without punishment for centuries. We have been denied the ability to love and cultivate healthy relationships with our men without being labeled as "thirsty" or "gold diggers". Society would rather rear up our young than allow us to lead, correct and guide them. **BLACK WOMEN** are incarcerated at alarming rates for petty crimes

14

while the wealthy and lighter race women receive a mere slap on the wrist for the same wrongdoings.

Our girls and are being robbed of their innocence well before puberty has a chance to begin. Forced to grow up sooner and act older than what they are physically and mentally. Young **BLACK WOMEN** are being lost, abducted in plain sight, yet you see no national uproar or initiatives put in place to save them. Our older women are disrespected and stepped upon like dirt, but no one comes to their defense.

These and many more crimes against **BLACK WOMEN** have been going on for years, but where is the public outcry? Where is the national state of emergency? Why are little black faces, in all of their innocence not plastered on our television screens during the nightly news? There is no new legislation being drafted to protect us like they are protecting those affected by opioid abuse. It seems that even in the year 2019, despite advanced technology, innovative discoveries and ground breaking milestones the world is sending a message loud and clear. That message is that the world does not care about and would be better off without the **Black Woman**!

We find her name being stricken out of the history books and even her greatest triumphs could not have been possible without the help of a man. Take Cleopatra for instance, in all her glory and power; history attributes all of her success to being a pale skinned woman with thin lips and European styled straight, silky hair. Despite the location of her kingdom being in a part of the world where no one of that complexion or hair texture exists. These are the lies they teach our children to believe! But why? Is there a reason a **BLACK WOMAN** cannot command an army of thousands to go to war at the snap of her finger? Is it that absurd to believe that Cleopatra, a woman of color, could not have tens of thousands of loyal subjects at her beckoning command, or have we just been reduced to eye rolls, multi colored weaves and having bad attitudes?  Why does the world hate **BLACK WOMEN** so? To get a better answer to this question I believe we must start at the beginning and study the anatomy of the most sought after being on this planet.

# The Magic Within

The anatomy of the **BLACK WOMAN** is very

important when studying the social injustices that are

experienced by us every day of our lives. The cast and

mold that God, our creator, used to make us is one that

has been replicated many times over, yet no plastic

surgeon can seem to come close to the natural beauty,

sophisticated charm and utter glory that is a **BLACK WOMAN**. I urge you Queen, to take a look down at your feet. No matter how big or small, no matter how wide or narrow, the feet of a **BLACK WOMAN** have the power to lead captives out of bondage. It is estimated that Harriet Tubman alone made at least nineteen trips back to the south and freed over 300 slaves during a ten year period of time. I can imagine Old Moses, as she was called, trudging hundreds of miles on foot through thick brush, muddy waters and stony ground. As she walked and perhaps sometimes even ran back and forth, back and forth with the soles of her shoes worn through and through. Her feet covered in blisters and the pain of fallen arches; she never gave in nor did she give up. She is quoted as saying that she could have freed hundreds more people had they only known that they were indeed slaves. Think of her feet, now look back at your own feet. Although your journey may be different from that of Harriet Tubman you must realize that your feet were made to lead the masses. Whether you are leading a church choir, a mentoring group for young **Black Girls**, a support group for women or even your own children. Pacing the floor in silent prayer and petition for a sick family member or loved one, or just trying to look cute in a pair of heels; remember each step you take is more powerful than you think.  That same tenacity and determination that drove Harriet Tubman, the brave heroine of her time, that she had found inside herself you too were born with.  Watch your step honey, but you MUST keep on *strutin'*!

Now make your way upward from your feet to your lower legs and knees.  This is the area of our bodies that we often neglect and mostly treat unkind.  Our knees take most of the impact and essentially carry our bodyweight.  An article published by The Arthritis Foundation states that for every pound that you are overweight it will add up to four times as much stress to your knees.  Shocking right?  That means that if you are ten pounds overweight you can expect up to forty extra pounds of stress added to your knees, and if you are a whopping one hundred pounds overweight, well you get the picture. The knees of the **BLACK WOMAN** are perhaps the strongest of all the joints in our body. Not because we are carrying extra weight from all of the good eating we are doing. It is no secret that the kitchen of the **BLACK WOMAN** produces some of the finest dishes that you would not be able to find in many five star restaurants. I say our knees are strong because of what we do with them. Taking a knee to look our children in the eye to encourage them and let them know just how proud we are of them or even bending them in submission to an all seeing and all-knowing wise and powerful God who delights in special alone time spent with His child. I can imagine the knees of my grandmother who worked hard to provide for four children all on her own. I can picture her praying and pleading with God not knowing how she would get by, but having faith and trusting in Him to know that He would see her through her darkest days. Anytime we square up to

21

tackle any head on battle that this world will throw our way, remember to fight less with your hands and your words and more on your knees. Life's hardest battles are fought on our knees, so if you have not made His hotline bling and consulted God in some time it is my sincere prayer that you start today. Imagine how happy he would be to hear from you!

Continuing our journey upward we come to a special place; the holy hips and thighs! The hips and thighs of a **BLACK WOMAN** carried the seed of humanity and gave birth to the world. You see after God had created man in His image. **PAUSE**... read that line again! God created man in His image, not man evolved from primate and took on the image of himself. You can choose to believe what you'd like but I know without a shadow of a doubt that I was made in the image of my Father in heaven. You may think you derived from a monkey and that is fine with me, but as for me and my household, we have a little bit better sense than that.

Let's continue, God created man in his image and saw that it was not right for man to be alone, he needed a help mate. He caused a deep sleep to fall upon the man and from him created Woman. The two lived together in a lush garden that God had prepared for them called Eden. In Eden, God made sure that the needs of both Man and Woman were met in the form of beautiful trees used for shade and they were also plenteous in food. The location of Eden is believed to be central Africa, southwest of the empire of Cush and present day Ethiopia. This is the part your oppressors choose to leave out! Now I am in no way nor do I claim to be a Bible or history scholar, however I do have a Ph.D. in common sense. I am so sensible that I know the land of Ethiopia is native to a peculiar people with darker skin, full lips and kinky hair (do you catch my drift?) Man called Woman by the name of Eve, which means "mother of all living." Eve a **BLACK WOMAN**, and the mother of all living gave birth to Cain, his brother Abel and later Seth, need I say more?

Considering that **BLACK WOMEN** carry most of their weight in more flattering places like the thighs and bosom I feel it is significant to discuss the strength of the shoulders. The shoulders of the **BLACK WOMAN** carry the weight of the world and I do mean that literally. They are not slouched or rolled inward but broad and straight, upright and supportive. These shoulders carry her children and provide them shelter from any tempest. One pivotal account of the Civil Rights Movement that I found astounding were events known as sit-ins. Men and women of color attempting to desegregate diners that only served white customers often shaming them to go to the back door when wanting to purchase food. These sit-ins often times ended very violently for those who participated, in fact, some were so violent that many parents refused to allow their children to participate in them at all. Non-violence was a huge concept of the movement, so when white patrons would pour scalding hot coffee or ice cold milk over the heads of those brave men and women what do you think those same shoulders did?  Did they fold under pressure?  Did they cave in defeat?  Absolutely not!  Those shoulders were thrown back, poised and erect and in the end we prevailed.

As a child I used to laugh at a story my grandmother used to tell me.  Growing up in Louisiana, her parents instilled the value of hard work and discipline in each of their eight children.  The family not only grew their own produce but even raised their own animals.  Many of their neighbors and friends would come to them to purchase from them rather than spend their hard earned money in stores ran by whites that treated them and their families with contempt.  An older white woman whose name flees my mind was one of their family's most loyal patrons.  The woman had a beautiful parrot that she kept perched in a cage outside her front door.  Anytime my grandmother or any one of her brothers or sisters came by to deliver her goods the parrot would alert its owner letting her know a guest was approaching the door.  He would holler, "*Nigga wanna* see you, *nigga*

*wanna* see you!"  Again as a child I thought it was funny,

not only did the bird talk but it was actually able to

differentiate race which I have no doubt was something

that it had been taught.

"I *woulda* knocked that cage over, Grannie," I

chuckled.

"It didn't bother me none," she would reply.  "In your

life you are going to get called many a names.  It's only when

you start to believe that you are the mean names that people

call you, that's when you have a problem."

As a young child I could not understand how she

could say something like that.  No one deserves to be

treated or talked to like that by a person, yet alone a

dumb old bird.  Twenty or so years later--I finally get it

Grannie!  I think back at how proud she was that she had

not let the mean-spiritedness of others get her down.  I

feel that same pride each and every time I look at my

reflection in the mirror and **BLACK WOMAN** you should too!

Perhaps the most important part of our DNA is the strong mind and determination that each and every **BLACK WOMAN** possesses. We were Kings and Queens stolen by cowards and spineless thieves with no religious or moral convictions from our native home. They packed us tightly into the clammy and musty bellies of cargo ships like livestock. Sent across a roaring blue yonder that stretched as far as the eye could see. Auctioned off on blocks for money, brutally raped and beaten, forced to work endless plow fields in treacherous weather conditions. Given the parts of the pig and cow that our oppressors dared not touch to feed our families. **BLACK WOMEN** adapted to this strange land and did not quiver up and die. They persevered, they flourished, they survived survived!

A crown of hair, whether it is curly, tightly coiled, loosely waved or bone straight is our glory. The hair of a

**BLACK WOMAN** is the most versatile hair in the world. When it comes to the braiding or styling of our hair the options are endless and others hate it! Being able to switch our look up at the drop of a dime and not being forced to go around with the same old plain Jane mundane look from day to day is enough to make anyone jealous. This is why our hair is more than likely gazed at like a sideshow attraction, it cannot be understood and duplicated so they find ways to slander and make fun of it. If I have learned one thing in my life it is that things that cannot be explained, tamed or reproduced are often labeled as weird or distracting. In the case of our hair, there is nothing weird or distracting about it, rock it and flaunt it!

Last but not least our beautiful, wonderful skin that shows just how much God was in His bag when he created us. Ranging from deep hues of purple to the fairest hints of yellow. Red and pink undertones that protect us from the harmful rays of sun. Many women use artificial spray tans to achieve what we were born with and rock everyday—how terrible that must be. The cells that secrete the melanin that gives us our color are the magic that the world wishes it could recreate. It cannot be harvested, bottled up and put into jars to be sold at outrageous markup prices. Naturally thick, full lips enclose our beautiful smiles. **BLACK WOMAN** you are that magic the world wishes it had!

Whew! Are you still with me? I am not sure about you but just writing this gave me chills. I stopped twice and began to dance wildly around my room because I had forgotten just how amazingly dope we are! I, like many of you need a gentle reminder, a little nudge, an encouraging push to help me tap into the greatness and potential I was born with! My dear *Sistah*, it is so easy to get distracted. It is so easy to forget how powerful you are. The day to day Monday through Friday nine to five hustle and bustle is enough to deter your mind from that. Then add in trying to raise children in a crooked and perverse world that is not set up for us to succeed, maintaining your marriage or current relationship, commitments with friends, detoxing, dieting, cutting negativity out of your life, making sure you eat right and your skin is glows flawlessly. Wash day for your natural hair, shampooing and conditioning, moisturizing and oiling, shaving—when do you have time to practice self-care or self-love?!

Despite the endless list of things that make us stand out and prove we are without a doubt a cut above the rest why does society tell us we are inferior? Why when we turn on the television do our children not see other children that look like they do? Why are normal, healthy **BLACK** families so scarce in media and television portrayals? Why is it so difficult to find a **BLACK** doll for our daughters to play with? The answer is simple, it is because the world knows that if we begin to be comfortable in our own skin that we cannot be bought or controlled. It is time we begin to live our lives as boldly and beautifully as we truly are.  This book will show you how to love yourself and not depend on society to show you love.  I declare that this year and every other year after it is the year of the **BLACK WOMAN** and we are here to stay!

# Day 1

## Eff Your Feelings, and Your Couch!

Many times as women, we are forced to put our own

feelings and agendas on the back burner. I can vividly recall

many nights lying in bed, body tired without an ounce of

energy to spare.  Physically and emotionally drained and then it hit me!  I forgot to do some random thing.  The thing I forgot to do varied from time to time and as long as the clock keep on ticking and the gray hairs keep sprouting, I fear it will only get worse.  I often think to myself, *"What the heck were you doing that you forgot to do that thing?"*  The answer is always the same; I was too busy doing everything else for everyone else that I had neglected to do this one thing for myself.  I know I am not alone.  Whether age plays a role in the forgetfulness of mind is not a contributing factor.  The bottom line is: it is very easy to get wrapped up in others and forget self.

Dave Chappelle, a world renowned stand-up comedian and actor has a career that spans decades.  He has starred in numerous comedy specials, blockbuster movies as well as his own self-titled comedy sketch show.  One of his most famous sketches to date was one where he did a rousing impersonation of the late funk singer Rick James.  The story was told by the late actor and brother of actor Eddie Murphy, Charlie. Charlie Murphy begins the story by describing the kind of relationship he and his brother shared with the late singer and song writer. It was a relationship filled with exotically wild parties riddled with heavy drug use. On one incidence Rick was described as stumbling into Eddie's apartment wearing a pair of heavily soiled platform shoes. Chappelle in costume as Rick James purposely drags his feet on the carpet of the plush apartment, leaving a trail of dirt and mud from the front door before dramatically flopping down on the actors' couch. Now this was not just any old couch, this was a very expensive white couch, in fact I distinctly remember the couch in the sketch being the whitest couch I had ever seen, so if you have not seen this particular sketch imagine that. After a war of words about the mess he had just made, James becomes irate and begins grinding his dirty feet into the couch while yelling, *" f yo couch!"*

Just the thought of the sketch tickles me and makes me laugh. While the disregard for Eddie Murphy's personal property was disrespectful, we must learn to possess the same attitude displayed by Rick James when it comes to putting others first at all times. Think about it, how many times have you sacrificed your own happiness just to please someone else? How many times have you neglected self to put the agenda of others before your own? For me this comes daily! The desire to say yes to avoid hurting anyone's feelings or to keep the peace often haunts me. Learning to say no is a concept we all must begin to get comfortable saying. Whether that's in the office, in our communities and yes, even in our own homes.

Do not let the poor planning or execution of others place you in a bind that you cannot financially or mentally recover from. We as **BLACK WOMEN** have been regarded as fixers. We are expected to get the job done by any means necessary despite any road blocks that may lie ahead. We are often the first sought out for advice when things do not go as planned but never receive the proper recognition in the end when the desired results have been attained. While this bad, a fixer attitude may be praised in the workplace and we must ensure we are getting the proper recognition we deserve for all of the outstanding talents we bring to the table. No matter the occupation, nor matter the pay grade we all have something to offer in our respective areas of employment. If it were not so we would not have that job or position.

Sometimes it is perfectly fine to say, *"f your feelings and your couch,"* in the form of the word "no!" No I cannot commit to this event because you gave me no prior notice! No, I cannot make something happen overnight that you could not pull off in a weeks' time! No! No! No!

Try saying the word no today. Your no does not mean you cannot accomplish the task, it simply means that in a conscious effort to maintain your sanity you must decline.  Anxiety and depression are two major contributors to many of the mental health disorders that plague the **Black** community, striking our women the hardest.  The stigma of seeking treatment or taking medications to counteract those feelings of helplessness has plagued us as a race for far too long. It is time we admit that we have a problem and seek treatment for these disorders.

If I could describe my friend Nomi I would say she is a lot like me.  Quiet and timid unless spoken to, a fairly active working mother of one daughter in her early thirties.  Nomi sat quietly at her desk one afternoon drumming her nails.  She had a distinct taste of salt in her mouth each time she swallowed.  Blaming it on her unhealthy choices of snack foods she had eaten from the vending machine.  She tried to ignore the taste until a slight headache crept upon her.  Being the poster child for fair health, perfect blood pressure and cholesterol she began to worry, something just did not feel right.

Hurrying over to her doctor's office after work, she was diagnosed with a tension headache related to unknown stressors. The treatment was simple, an injection for the pain and a low dose anti-anxiety medication; Nomi declined the treatment, thinking that these symptoms would let up on their own and resolve itself without intervention. Soon after her sleep cycle became irregular, a red flag for her because she was one to fall asleep at the drop of a dime, especially during a long car ride. It became so irregular that she soon found it hard to sleep at all. Taking advice from family and friends she tried many different remedies such as herbal teas, essential oils and briefly tried meditation all which offered her little to no relief. As the days turned into weeks and weeks into months her symptoms never seemed to get any better. The headaches were now constant, continuous and they never stopped. She began experiencing heart palpitations, rapid breathing and a feeling of tightness in her chest. When asked to describe these feelings to me she stated it felt like she was trapped in a tiny room with little to no oxygen, knowing soon if you did not escape you were certain to meet demise.

During this time her social interactions spiraled downhill, she retreated from public outings with friends and often ran away from conversations with others, not knowing what or whom would trigger a pending anxiety attack. Nomi decided she had finally had enough, she could not live like that anymore. She returned to her healthcare professional and submitted to medical treatment for an anxiety disorder to include daily medication for the condition.

Nomi now manages her anxiety with a daily medication regime and now has a new outlook on life. "I remember feeling hopeless," she said with tears in her eyes. "I felt the only way I could escape these feelings were if I died and I did not want that." She is now back to her old self, loud, slightly annoying (I mean that with love) and more outgoing and ambitious as ever. Her advice is simple, "See a doctor if you are battling anxiety, depression or any other form of mental illness!" Nomi admits being a **BLACK WOMAN** taking medicine for a mental disorder is still hard for some to understand. Being referred to as crazy never gets easy but she now has something that perhaps even her biggest critics do not—peace of mind!

"Being the only **BLACK WOMAN** at my job, I've always felt like I had to compete twice as hard to show my worth," she states. "I felt like I had to be the first one to get there in the morning and the last one to leave every night. I've done more work in one week than others do in one day."

"Work often traveled home with me many nights while my supervisors slept comfortably or enjoyed family time with their loved ones."

"I had to say no more!"

Nomi's confidence and work ethic has soared since she has been on her medication. While individual results with taking these types of medicines may vary, a great ending can be found in her story. Say no more to things that are beyond your control. Say no more to relationships where you give your all and get nothing in return. Say no more to the things that do not bring you joy and the happiness that you deserve! Despite what others may think or how they may feel, sometimes you simply have to say **NO!**

# Day 2

## You Are Fly

Nothing compliments my feature more than a pair of

freshly waxed, threaded or arched eyebrows.  Even with the

best makeup coverage, if my brows are off it seems my

entire face is off. Keeping up with the latest trends in beauty and fashion are a necessary part of my life, but like me I am sure you too get up some days just not feeling it. You lack the extra effort it takes to highlight, contour and play up those features. Come on, don't roll your eyes now, I know I cannot be the only one who gets a chronic case of the Monday Blues on Wednesday? Can I? Though I make it my business to engage in some sort of rigorous activity at least once a day, most days I would just prefer to buy a bigger shirt or a larger sized pair of jeans. Yes, my outward appearance is very important but it does not define who I am. So strong, beautiful **BLACK WOMAN** reading this, your outward appearance does not define you either.

While makeup and the latest fashion trends help to adorn the outer body your true beauty should radiate from within. So many times we as **BLACK WOMEN** are viewed as or come off to some as cold, hard and heartless. It is a condition we have been conditioned to emulate from years of psychological trauma and learned toxic behaviors. Well today is the day we call these unhealthy traits out, today these detestable acts stop!

In my younger years if you were to ask someone to describe me in a single word, most would associate me as being mean or always having an attitude. By the end of high school I had been called out of my name so much that I began to wear that name as more a badge of honor than the insult it was meant to be. Being known as this unflattering name was supposed to mean something to others that came in contact with me. It was supposed to mean that I did not tolerate any funny business; that I was less likely to be lied to, lied on or even taken advantage of. It was supposed to mean that no one would dare try me---but that is not what happened.

Being mean to people did not stop me from having my own feelings hurt in return and it certainly did not stop me from having my generosity and kindness in other areas to be taken for weakness. The reason being is because bad things happen to both good and bad

44

people. Now, if you agree why waste your time being a bitter and angry **BLACK WOMAN**? When you harbor bitterness and anger, in even just one tiny part of your body, it metastasizes. That means it spreads rapidly throughout your body infecting even the most delicate and wholesome parts of your inner being. Areas in your life where peace once resided are soon infected by this debilitating plague and before you know it you are a walking wasteland of bad language, bad manners and a bad decisions. It permeates into your relationships with your spouse or significant other, your children and even other family members and friends. I am sorry to be the one to have to break it to you darling, but there is not enough makeup in the world to cover up an ugly, resentful and bitter soul. The rarest gems and purest golden jewelry cannot beautify an ugly soul.

Last summer I did a seven day apology tour for all of my social media followers. While it may have seemed like a nice gesture, it was really seven days of me poking fun at my brothers and some of my friends.  Each day I would post a new video of me apologizing for some random mean thing that I had once done but I always found a way to turn it around on the person I was supposed to be apologizing to.  While this was done all for fun and games an apology tour in its true essence is not a bad idea.  Think about it, sitting down to acknowledge someone whom you know you have wronged. Acknowledging the fault and how it made you feel then closing it out by saying I forgive you, let's move forward.  I don't know how you feel about it, but I know a few people who owe me apologies and I may never get them.  So instead of me waiting around for them to get the courage to admit their wrong doings I choose to gladly to do it for them.

Some of you have been holding on to jealousy and hatred for so many years that it is almost second nature to harbor bad feelings, but where has it gotten you?  Did it help you get that good job, did it help you get that nice car that you ride around in?  Or is it the reason your blood pressure stays out of whack or the reason you toss and turn at night instead of sleeping peacefully?  When you choose to let go of the bitterness and hate that you have built up you allow your inner beauty to show.  Outward looks and appearances fade away, but a good heart and clean spirit stay young forever.

Let it shine so brightly that those you come in contact with cannot help but to take notice and say, "Hey I want what she's got!"  The older you get the less likely you will rely on your looks to take you places.  This absolutely does not mean that you don't still have it because *uhhh* BLACK DON'T CRACK (shots fired)!  Along with your looks you will have a better outlook on life and a clearer conscience.  Let us all try to as much as we possibly can show no ill will towards any of our *Sistahs*, it's a cold world we are living in but there is warmth in numbers!

Have you ever bounced back from a situation or illness that you thought would rob you of everything you had? For me it was a relationship. I had spent so many years pouring into this cup that I thought was a forever relationship only to find that there was a hole in the bottom of that cup. During those years there were so many promises made, so many opportunities passed by and sacrifices made only for it to crumble and fall to pieces right in front of my face. No amount of money could give me back what I had lost—my dignity and my self-respect. The hours, days, months and years that I wasted on his one person would never be returned to me.

"How would I ever come back from this", I cried to my mother. "I will never find another love like this again!"

The lie detector proved, that was a lie! In a period of nine months I put my life back together piece by piece. I harbored a lot of hatred for that one person who had broken my heart. The thought of him mad my blood boil and if anyone asked me about him they received an ear full. I had spent so much time hating everything about him that allowed myself to get lost in that bitterness. All five feet nine inches of me were polluted with unclean and impure thoughts. So many opportunities passed me by, so many blessings and breakthroughs alluded me because I could not find it in my heart to forgive.

As I unpacked my feelings, my hurt and disappointment in love, at the bottom of a box I found a little glimmer of hope that twinkled like the sun. It was the self-realization that although I had terrible luck in relationships, I was a good person. A good person with good intentions and a good heart. How could anyone not love me? Why would anyone not want to love me? The moment I stopped feeling sorry for myself and realized who I was and what I was made of, those feelings of hopelessness left. I dated again, a few times after that to be exact and although those relationships did not last, I never looked at myself the same again.

Bitterness begets bitterness just as hatred begets hatred. Imagine having a host of talent stored up in your body that you cannot use it because your bitter attitudes makes it impossible for you to work with others? How much better would your life be if you chose to let go of all concealed animosity in your heart? Just as dangerous toxins can pollute your entire body so can those two attitudes. If left untreated they can take root and choke the very life right out of your body. I am not sure how you feel about it, but I have too much promise to be consumed by anything other than positivity. This change can be attained but it is a choice that you will have to come to on your own. Resolve in your heart and mind today that you will live a life of promise and not of bitterness.

# *Day 3*

## *Finding the Dopeness Within*

Searching your inner most being find what makes you

unique.  This may require you to reach out to close friends or

perhaps even your family just to get their opinion of what they feel your best qualities are. *Dopeness* is more than a made up word or feeling, it is an overall sense of self-worth and accomplishment. While you may be fighting to keep your marriage or relationship alive there are those that are having to come to the shocking conclusion that theirs is over. There is someone out there that wishes they had what you currently have, no matter how much or how little. There is someone out there who wishes they could be in your shoes, no matter how new or worn they are, there is always someone else that is worse off than you. Yes, you may feel as if you have hit rock bottom but rest assured that for so many others it is a lot worse.

So many women are fighting silent battles that no one knows anything about. There are no neon lights affixed to the top of heads flashing hazardous caution signs to let you know that your co-worker is suffering from depression. Feelings of depression are usually brought on by feelings of uselessness or defeat. These feelings are different than seasonal depression that is brought on by large gatherings during the holidays, or perhaps the anniversary of the death of a loved one or past traumatic event.  The type of depression I speak of can come from our own feelings of worthlessness or verbal and physical abuse.  In these cases somewhere along the line a person has lost that sense of being a dope individual.  We all have dope qualities within, but how do we find them?

Buried deep down inside of you lies something that makes you who you are. Whether it is a laugh, a gorgeous smile or a good sense of humor.  We all have at least one quality that makes us stand out from the crowd.

# Find it!  Cultivate it!

# Harvest it!  Use it!

So many of you are sitting on a gold mine of ideas and talents that are just waiting to be brought to the light.  One of the main things that stops us from pushing through to the next level is this little thing called fear.  Fear is no stranger, you've heard its voice before, it says things like, *"you don't look like a model,"* or *"your idea for a business will never get off of the* ground," and so on and so forth. Fear is the weed that chokes the roots of a beautiful flower preventing it from blooming. That flower can be a host of different things; your business, your next project or your dream job. I say enough is enough! I challenge each and every one of you reading this book to stop living in the spirit of fear and go out and get what belongs to you! How can you know if you will ever succeed if you do not first try? One small step is all it takes.

Finding your *dopeness* is only half of the battle beloved, once you find it, it is a must that you use it. There is no sense in exploring the depths of your soul to retrieve this rare treasure only to proudly display it on a shelf to collect dust. It should never be used for show and tell or on certain occasions, oh no my Queen. That *dopeness* should be seen in your daily walk and if you use it correctly it should shine from miles away. They should see you coming from down the road like, *"Hey, there goes that Sistah!"* Yes it is okay to flaunt your stuff, but only a true Queen knows the right stuff to flaunt!

# Day 4

## Be A Regular Milkshake

Being myself was something I always found hard to do and for many reasons. I have a feeling many other women especially those of color have a hard time doing this as well because the world does not like us as our natural selves. New laws and legislation have recently been passed making it illegal for employers to discriminate against potential employees based on their natural hairstyles! I don't think you understand the magnitude of that last sentence, so allow me to repeat. In 2019, a law had to be passed to allow us to wear our hair in natural protective styles in the workplace! This contradicts the familiar phrase we have all heard time and time again imploring us to just be ourselves. How? How can I be myself if I can potentially lose my job because of the way my hair naturally grows out of my head? We were taught that if certain people did not like us for who we were then they were not worthy of being called a friend. Yet many of us found ourselves acting a certain way or liking certain things all because others we associated with liked them.

Stacy was about three year's older than I was. We were not supposed to meet that year in high school. We did not like the same things and we certainly did not have the same social crowds. In my youth I was very childish and immature as a young teen often is, but Stacy was getting ready to go off to college, she was focused, she was driven and she was determined, I was just there to have a good time. In my sense of having a good time I listened to and believed certain things that probably shouldn't have warranted my attention or time. I was told many terrible, ugly, and mean things about Stacy. My small circle of friends did not like her and if I wanted to remain true and loyal to them I was not to like her either. As stated before, Stacy and I were not supposed to ever be in that space together, but by divine appointment, there we were…together. That year Stacy taught me so much. She calmed me down and made me realize that I had so much more life to live and so much more potential than I was willing to give myself credit for. Stacy was loyal, she was dependable, she never lied to me, she never had me out there looking stupid, Stacy never stole from me-- she was a better friend to me than many of my other so called friends were. Stacy was the true friend that I never expected and never deserved.

Have you ever heard of a unicorn milkshake? Do no fret if you haven't, I had no clue what one was until my daughters showed me a video of one being made. While the seemingly magical concoctions can vary in ingredients let me describe the one I saw being made as a treat for a child's birthday party. First you begin with a regular sized mason jar. In a blender combine your desired flavor of ice cream along with any flavored syrups and milk. After the mixture is blended to a drinkable consistency pour it into the jar. Take a few pieces of fresh fruit and skewer them to create a decorative garnish—but wait, there's more!

Next take your favorite chocolate candy bar and crush it up into small bite sized pieces, sprinkling them on top of your blended milkshake. With a knife, spread a thick layer of cake frosting all around the rim of the glass. No need to be neat or tidy, just slather it on, you will see why in just a second. Break up pieces of your favorite flavor cotton candy, adhere it to the rim of the glass using the frosting as glue to secure it and hold it in place. Any gaps along the rim where the icing can still be seen fill in with small pieces of any fruity or chocolate bite sized candy. Pile the whipped cream high above the rim of the glass. Top with your choice of cookie that would best compliment your milkshakes flavor. If you want to be extra, take miniature chocolate candy bars and stick it into the whipped cream for height. Take a plastic straw and coat it heavily in frosting; stick more pieces of cotton candy along it for decoration and finally garnish with sprinkles!

# What the hell!

Just thinking about this runs my blood sugar up! What happened to the good old days when a milkshake was a simple blend of ice cream and milk garnished with a cherry on top? Wouldn't you rather have a plain old milkshake as opposed to this puffed up, over glorified and terribly unhealthy version of one any day of the week? Just as the unicorn milkshake and its many components, some people come with just as many attitudes, personalities and traits. In this situation wouldn't you rather be a regular milkshake?

In this age of over indulgence in foods, clothing and even body types, finding the time to be anything other than yourself can be exhausting. Keeping up with the fads and trends should not be so much a part of your life that you lose the essence of who you really are. There is nothing wrong with making small lifestyle changes to promote health , wellness and an overall better quality of life, however if your lifestyle changes affect your livelihood to the point that you don't know whether you're coming or going is it really doing you any good?

Take the lesson I learned with Stacy as your guide. Do not be afraid to go against the grain or to be different. We were all made differently for a reason, embrace it. Do you remember how disgusted Becky and her friend were in the beginning of Sir Mix A Lot's "Baby Got Back" video? Now we are seeing trends where Becky and her friends all want the same big hips, thighs and the junk in the trunk we were born with. It is so bad that these women are going to extreme measures just to look like something they once all shamed us for. We, **BLACK WOMEN,** are the prototype! We are the

Holy Grail and the apple of all of their eyes! We are the cream of the crop, the crème de la crème; a holy trifecta wrapped up into one.

So why hide the things that make us different or the things that cause us to stand out? It is human nature to respond to things that we do not understand with opposition, and unfortunately Becky's entire family has been doing that and holding those things against us for far too long. So what you're a girl that likes anime or likes to read comic books. Somewhere down the line you were told that while your natural skin tone is nice you would be so much prettier if you were lighter and maybe if your hair was straighter you would be accepted and perhaps not looked over for that promotion. **Somewhere, somehow, somebody told a damn lie!** There is no getting around the fact that in the eyes of many we will not be counted as being attractive, so what, that's their loss. It really burns my grits when I hear Black Men talking down and badly **about BLACK WOMEN** and how they do not date them, that's another book in its own that I am not qualified to write, but attacking our own is something we all need to learn to stop doing.  Regardless of preference I am a firm believer that there is someone out there for everyone.  Someone is out there who loves anime and comic books just as much as you do.  Just like there is someone out there who loves your dark skin and kinky hair.  So in this world of unicorn milkshakes, dare to be a regular milkshake, just be yourself!

# *Day 5*

## *A Beautiful Mess*

The term beautiful is rarely found in the same sentence as the word mess and for very obvious reasons. Beautiful is a term of endearment and affection while the term mess is used to describe anything other than just that. A mess is something repulsive and something we would prefer to keep out of sight and out of mind. Through this journey it is important to remember that every day will not be easy, everyday moment will not be glitter and every one will NOT cheer you on or congratulate you with a shower of confetti. To be quite honest there are many days ahead that will simply be a mess, your goal is to find the beauty within.

The easiest way I can describe this process is with this simple exercise. Clear your mind of all of the distractions as you continue to read this book. Take a moment to reflect on your life in its present state. Ponder on things that are going right, the things that have gone left, the good, the bad and the in between. No matter the current state of your life, how big or small your problems may be, always remember there is someone out there who is worse off than you are. Hard to imagine, huh? Although everything may be going wrong in your life, think about others who for some reason have no home to live in. There are an alarming number of people who are living out of their cars right now at this very moment but many of you are fortunate enough to have a roof over your head at night. There are millions of people who have to rely on places like gas stations for food and nourishment because it is all that they can afford.

I recently had a discussion with a close friend named Princess. She had found herself in an unbelievable situation. I do not wish to share the details of her story for others to try to figure out who she is, but so that we can learn from it. There is no doubt in my mind that many will read this book having felt like or are currently feeling like she did when her husband left her.

"One day my husband stopped coming home," she said. "One or two nights here and there, then one day he came home for the last time. As I woman naturally I blamed myself, the man I had kept myself up for, kept a clean house for, raised children for had the nerve to tell me through text that he had fallen out of love with me."

The news was unsettling for me to hear and very hard to process. In my personal opinion Princess had always gone above and beyond for her family. If there was no hope for her then surely there was no hope for any of us. She continued, "I had spent years making sure I was put together for my husband and he still left."

In the worlds way of thinking I can see how it would be easy to put the blame solely on Princess for her failed marriage. Perhaps if she had spent more time tending to the needs of her husband instead of making sure she was dressed nicely and her home was clean her marriage would have worked.

# Hell nah!

Ladies, just like Princess' husband you cannot keep a man that does not want to be kept! If you feel as if you have to prance around in the best clothes and a full face of makeup to keep him you are sadly mistaken. Face it, every day will not be a full face makeup day. Every day will not be a designer heels and bag day and that is perfectly fine. No one is saying you have to have it all together all of the time.

It took a while and some very stern talking to and now I can hardly recognize Princess. Not because she has let herself go, but she has finally let herself live. She has lost weight and is making healthier choices about her lifestyle. Princess is never home, always on the go and on the move. It is so refreshing to see this new side of her and the new life she is choosing to live in spite of everything that has happened. She did not choose to live in self-pity and loathe in her misery. For years, being married had denied her of her happiness and I am so glad she has found her happy place with or without a man!

"I was a mess Abril," she yelled at me through the phone. "When he left I kept trying to figure out what I did wrong. I begged him to stay, I told him I would change, I promised to do whatever he wanted me to do."

"Being alone for the first time in twenty-two years was hard, but I found the beauty in my mess!"

# Day 6

## I Forgive Me

Earlier in this book we touched on forgiveness of others for their wrongdoings. However the type of forgiveness being discussed here will specifically be for your benefit. You may be thinking to yourself, "Why do I need forgiveness?" Again, I am so glad you asked! Have you ever:

- Put yourself in a terrible or dangerous position physically, mentally, financially, or emotionally knowing damn well you should not have?

- Taken the blame for something you did not do because you did not want to see the responsible party hurt?

- Settled for something or someone that was way out of your league?

- Believed that you were not good enough in your own mind or because someone told you that you weren't?

- Dumbed yourself down to fit in with a particular crowd?

- Refrained from speaking up in a matter that you knew in your heart was wrong or unfair and later felt convicted?

- Missed out on opportunities for advancement and or promotion because of fear?

I could continue this list but if you answered yes to any of these questions then yes, this applies to you. Some of you are stuck in the positions you are in because of the extra weight and baggage you are holding onto in the form of hate and grudges has been forgiven of the trespasser but not of yourself. Your promotion, your elevation and your advancement to the next level are all tied down because you have never told yourself that you were sorry.

Playing the victim is an easy thing to do but that does not mean that responsibility stops there!

Give yourself the permission to apologize to yourself for all the things you let slide. Many of you have patiently waited for someone to see your self-worth and treat you accordingly. You have bent over backwards for so many people over the years without so much as a thank you in return. How many of you have prayed endless nights for your relationship to turn around and it did not? Come on, be honest, I can't be the only one that has a couple hundred failed engagements under her belt? How many of you have toughed it out in a relationship, hoping that one day it would turn around in your favor? How many of you have wasted time and energy that you can never get back, pouring love, care and devotion into a person that sucked the life out of you? These are just a few of the things we for certain need to forgive ourselves for. One thing is for certain, we are all guilty of holding on to something or someone who has meant us no earthly good!

I love that phrase! It is not just something that your grandma used to utter to add emphasis to her argument, it carries a lot of weight behind it. Think for just a second of this beautiful world we live in. I will not give you a Sunday School lesson but we all know the story of creation and of how the heavens and the Earth were created. How God in all of His wisdom, power and majesty simply spoke a word and it was done. After God had finished his creating, He looked over all that he had made. I imagine he did this proudly, with His chest poked out and declared that everything He had created was good. Then came sin, in the form of deception and greed and from that moment on all of the good that God had just created was undone. As we look at the news and all of the injustices that surround us in this lifetime we can clearly see that there is a limited amount of good left in the world. You have to look hard to find it, if you're in a hurry you will pass right on by the good in the world.

My commute to work is anything less than spectacular. I pass the same rundown buildings and the same people day after day, nothing really catches my eye. One day as I was driving in I glanced up at the sky. The way the pinks and blues and yellows and oranges blended together was strikingly beautiful to me. In that moment I realized that God had created this morning especially for me to enjoy. I marveled at his handiwork in the sky, how many of us are so busy that we rarely have time to marvel at the beautiful masterpieces that God has hand created just for us to enjoy? I know I am guilty of that, so now everyday on my commute I am sure to stop and pause and thank God for His creation. No matter if the sun is or not I have learned to stop and admire the beauty that God has set before me to enjoy, I implore you, to do the same. Take time from your busy day to stop and admire the beauty that God has set here in front of you.

On a more personal note I love flowers almost as much as the next girl. Not the flowers that are pre-grown and you dig a hole and plant to add color to your landscape. I love planting seasonal bulbs. The joy in watching a bulb sprout forth from nothing into something beautifully unknown is very special to me. Planting bulbs is not for the faint at heart or the impatient of which I possess both traits. After weeks of watering I expect to see some sort of progress, but unfortunately these bulbs did not work on my time. They did not bloom when I said bloom, they have a process to undergo.

Just as the bloom undergoes a process before sprouting out into something aesthetically gorgeous, believe it or not so do you. You did not wake up this morning having it all together. In fact, someone went to bed last night with the sink full of unwashed dishes, a pile of laundry on the couch and without their protective bonnet on their heads...and that is okay! Am I in your neighborhood yet? In many ways we all require some form of nurture and care in order to put our best foot forward. When Beyonce' said, "I woke up like this," the entire world went crazy and rightfully so. What she did not say was that she woke up like this each and every day of her life! You very well may wake up flawless every once in a blue moon but please do not sell yourself short in thinking you must wake up flawless every day. No one wakes up in the greatest of moods every day. For many, becoming a fully functioning adult does not kick in until their third or fourth cup of coffee. No one wakes up with every hair in place and without a trail of dried slobber formed in the corner of their mouth. If no one wakes up like this on a consistent basis why should you?

Like the flower you too must undergo the proper nurturing and care in order to blossom and bloom to our fullest potential. If you know anything about gardening you will know that a seed will not sprout in just any old kind of soil. Tossing seeds in unnourished soils is the same as writing with a pencil with no point. Seeds are planted in fertile soil so that they have the best chance to grow. They need to be in the proper environment. You too need to be rooted and planted in the right kind of soil. If your current relationship with your significant other, friends, or your job is holding you back from taking that next big step; you have outgrown that pot and need to be replanted.  If that job is hindering you from getting that promotion that you are over qualified for then you my dear too have outgrown that pot and need to be replanted.

It is very important that the people you allow in your life are depositing nourishing thoughts, actions and energy into your soil. Protecting your peace and your joy are vital in this process of growth.  If what you are doing is not bringing you joy then you will only grow to loathe that very thing.  Protect your peace of mind my *Sistah,* protect your sense of security my Queen and most of all protect your joy at all times at all costs—even if that means cutting ties with close friends and family.  Yes, I said family!  All family *ain't family*; and if you choose to keep it real with yourself you will know I *ain't lyin'*!  If family no longer serves a purpose in your life, if family is not helping you grown and move forward, if family is not celebrating the highs and can only seem to remember the lows, do not be afraid to leave them right where they had you f'd up at!

# Day 7

## Know Your Worth

If I were to hand you a one hundred dollar bill, what would its value be? If you guessed one hundred dollars you are correct. What if I balled that same one hundred dollar bill up, stomped on it, spit on it and handed it to you, would you still accept it? Most would answer yes and rightfully so. Although that one hundred dollar bill has been crumbled up, stepped and spit on its value never changed. If the value of a piece of money never changes despite the things it has been through. My Sistah's, why do we allow the value in ourselves to change despite our circumstances?

I know you have been put through hell. Much like the money, you have had your feelings crumbled up, your happiness stomped out and in return for your kindness have had your face spat in. Even still your value does not change! What one person refuses to appreciate another person will. Your value is not determined by how you have been treated in the past but how you overcame that treatment. Your value is not determined by how much you have been used and abused by others but by how you were able to come out of that situation. No matter how many times you have been mistreated you are still priceless! No matter how many times you have been told that you do not matter, you do! Every now and then we have to shake off the negativity that has been thrown our way so that we can see our full potential. Your ideas have value and so do your thoughts.

When we are giving something of rare value, our first goal is to protect it with all of our might. Whether it be a piece of jewelry, a keepsake or a photograph we go out of our way to protect that item from the elements and from others. When the latest and greatest cell phone comes out we guard and protect that thing like it is a newborn infant. We buy fancy cases that are sold on the idea that it will protect our phones through whatever. You are of much more value than a piece of technology that is here today and gone tomorrow. Treat yourself accordingly! Demand that others treat you accordingly!

# Thoughts

So you've reached the end of the book, now what? Here is where the real work begins. There is no quick fix to self-love, in fact any journey to self-love is not a concept that can be done in seven steps and you are fixed forever. Quite the opposite, it is something you have to practice every day of your life, day by day and step by step. The steps do not have to be followed in order, you may very well run into a day where the lessons learned in day seven apply to your day one situation. Regardless, whatever the step is that you are on it is most important that you do not become stagnant in your daily walk towards a better, happier and healthier you. The relationships you will foster as a result of the love that you will find in yourself will amaze you.

Self-love is more candlelit baths and a bottle of wine, it is more than body scrubs and burning sage. Self-love is a concept that has been denied to **BLACK WOMEN** for ages. We are expected to care for, fight for and value others before we do those very same things for ourselves. Once this toxic cycle shows up at your own front door what will you do? The goal of this book is to break the cycle of the often depicted angry **BLACK WOMAN**. You have seen her being portrayed on the television shows and movie screens. Her mouth is a force that cannot be tamed, she says the first thing that comes to mind in every situation and never bites her tongue. We have all laughed at her, laughed with her, some of us are her. It is so amusing how the world loves to mimic the depictions of the angry **BLACK WOMAN** while simultaneously hating the **BLACK WOMEN** they interact with daily.

Breeding a future generation of angry **BLACK WOMEN** is not my goal. When I think of the future, I think of a world where the **BLACK WOMAN** is appreciated, nurtured and loved. A future where we are taken seriously, our opinions are valued and we are respected. The vision first begins with you and I. So, **BLACK WOMAN** I urge you to take charge of your happiness, take charge of youR joy but most of all love yourselves because if you don't, nobody else will.

Peace